One Person,
One Vote

One Person,
One Vote

How Changing
Our Voting System
Will Get Us Out of the
Mess We're In

W. R. Wilkerson III

Ciro's
BOOKS

For Al Gore,
who won the presidency of the United States
through national voting in November 2000
but was not allowed to take office

4152 Meridian Street, #6
Bellingham, WA 98226
888-88-CIROS
www.cirosbooks.com

ORDERING INFORMATION
Quantity sales. Special discounts are available on quantity purchases by corporations, associations, and others. For details, contact the "Special Sales Department" at the address above.

Orders by U.S. trade bookstores and wholesalers. Please contact BCH: Tel: (800) 431-1579; Fax (914) 835-0398.

Printed in the United States of America

Cataloging-in-Publication Data
Wilkerson, W R.
  One person, one vote : how changing our electoral system will get us out of the mess we're in / W. R. Wilkerson III.
    p. cm.
  Includes bibliographical references and index.
  ISBN 978-1-934499-00-9
1. Voting—United States. 2. Elections—United States. 3. Election law—United States. 4. Representative government and representation— United States. 5. Proportional representation—United States. 6. Apportionment (Election law)—United States. I. Title.
JF1075.U6 W55 2008
328.730734720—dc22   2007937929

Cover design: Bookwrights
Design & Composition: Beverly Butterfield, Girl of the West Productions
Copyediting: PeopleSpeak

SECOND EDITION
12 11 10 09 08   10 9 8 7 6 5 4 3 2 1

CONTENTS

PREFACE

Does your vote count? Are you sure? I'm not.

We all complain about the government. We all have strong opinions about taxes, illegal immigration, high gas prices, and two current wars that show no signs of ending. Had we the people been able to vote on all these key issues, they would have been resolved long ago. But we don't get to vote on them; we're allowed to vote only for politicians—who don't seem to get around to solving the problems that face us. We don't vote to elect members of the Supreme Court, we don't get to decide on issues such as gun control or same-sex marriage, and we certainly don't get to vote for tax reform, though I'll bet a lot of us would like to.

I wrote this book for two reasons. The first is my frustration over the presidential election of 2000. Al Gore clearly won the national vote by over 400,000 votes, but in presidential elections, the popular vote is not the one that counts. Our votes were hijacked by the Supreme Court, which made a decision for us and ruled five to four that George W. Bush was to be the forty-third president of the United States. A president of the United States was voted into office with only five votes. What happened to the other 105 million votes?[1]

The second reason I wrote this book is because of the terrible apathy too many Americans feel about elections. If given the chance, Americans love to vote. In 2007, 74 million votes were cast in the finale of *American Idol*. But when it comes to national elections, many people don't bother because they don't believe their votes really matter.

My son, who is in his early twenties, does not vote. When I ask him why he doesn't, his reply is always the same: "My vote doesn't count." And to a great degree, he is right. People are staying away from the polls because they look around and see that key decisions are being made by the few, rather than by the millions. They believe that their votes are worthless when a few people can overturn their decision later.

What's the solution? How can we change our broken system?

Americans are smart enough to figure out a path for our country, to know how to move forward past the endless debates about abortion, gun control, free speech, universal healthcare, terrorism, taxation, immigration, the national debt, and more. Isn't it time we had a real voice in these issues instead of sending someone to Washington to get stuck in the continual wrangling and to add layers of "pork" to every bill for the benefit of special interests?

National voting, sometimes called direct democracy, would give us that voice, and in this book I'll lay out my recipe for change and explain how national voting would work. Keep in mind that this book is only the very first step. We'll need to work together to construct a national voting system piece by piece. My goal is to start a national conversation. Once we agree that national voting will get our country out of the mess it's in, we can work out all the details. After all, we've had our Constitution for over two hundred years and we're still tinkering with it. If I tried to cover every possibility here, *One Person, One Vote* would be about nine hundred pages long and very technical. I want to inspire you, not bore you with a lot of fine print.

In the second half of the book you'll get a chance to try national voting for yourself and vote on thirty-one important issues facing our country today. Once national voting is in place, it will probably be impractical to vote on such a large number of issues in a single election. I'm including so many issues here because I want every one of you to find at least a few that you care passionately about. And I want you to discover for yourself that national voting can settle issues of all kinds—questions about government, citizens' rights and responsibilities, personal liberty, taxes and spending, international issues, law and order, and even life and death issues. For each issue, you'll read a summary of both sides, pro and con. Then you can decide for yourself where you stand. That's what democracy means.

I've included a sample ballot so you can express your opinions on all these issues and mail your ballot to the White House.

In the appendices you'll find a list of online resources that will help you learn more, as well as information on how to get in touch with your elected officials.

Throughout the book you'll find true stories—from our history and more recent times—about elections that were very, very close. Important issues and races were decided by tiny margins—often as little as a single vote. Some people might think this is a contradiction. Who cares about squeaker elections decided by a handful of votes? If our votes can be overturned by a judge, they believe, then voting is just a waste of time. But I passionately believe in voting, and I think that deep down most Americans do too.

This book is about why we need more voting, not less. We desperately need national voting, and until we can make it a reality, we have to keep voting every chance we get. Be inspired by these stories. Your vote does matter. That's why the people in power keep trying to take it away from you.

W. R. WILKERSON III
February 2008

PART ONE

National Voting

Power to the People

Why do so many of us feel disenfranchised and disconnected from our government? The answer is simple. Our political system does not work for us. It does not hear our voices. Over and over we have tried going to the polls and casting ballots on issues we feel passionate about. We have celebrated when our measure "won"—only to see it overturned by a single judge who was appointed, not voted into office. So we don't bother to vote anymore. Why should we when our votes don't count?

But what if we took the power back and made decisions for ourselves? What would our country be like? What would our lives be like?

1

It's Time for
a Second
American Revolution

The U.S. electoral system is broken beyond repair—let's throw it out and start over! Does that solution sound too radical? Consider the system we have now.

First, in close elections, nearly half the voters end up with elected officials who don't represent their views. In an electoral system where one candidate wins and all the others lose, a lot of people really have no representation in Congress, their state legislatures, and the governor's office—because they didn't vote for the winning candidate. Only the winner gets a voice—even when that winner earned less than half the votes cast in a race involving three or more candidates.

Second, unlike in most of the civilized world, legitimate third parties have no real voice. In a winner-take-all voting system, as we have in most of the United States, tremendous pressure is put on third-party candidates not to mount campaigns—and on voters not to vote for them—because they're seen as "spoilers" who allow other candidates to take office without a majority vote. This system excludes creative and original thinkers who can provide real solutions to our nation's problems. And it restricts the choices of the people who want to vote their consciences.

Third, many people in the United States vote with paperless electronic machines that cannot be trusted to count votes accurately or be free of tampering. You'll read more about this issue in chapter 5.

Finally, because of the way campaigns are funded, elected officials are captives of the corporate special interests who pay for their campaigns. Our representatives see themselves as accountable to private interests, not to the people who elected them.

Even when it works, our current electoral system has serious problems:

- The process of crafting legislation has been kidnapped by special interests. Even simple, straightforward changes get bogged down in the endless process of inserting favors to special interests and "earmarking" pet projects that have nothing to do with the issue at hand.
- So many amendments get inserted into bills that the policy goals are often lost.
- The bills themselves can run to hundreds or even thousands of pages. Nobody has time to read them, and legislators don't always know exactly what they're voting on.
- Wrangling over compromises keeps the real issues off the table. They don't get voted on, and the problems don't change.

WE THE PEOPLE DON'T BOTHER TO VOTE

The United States has some of the lowest election participation rates in the world. People think their votes don't matter, so they don't bother voting. Of the 142 million people who were registered to vote in the 2004 presidential election, 11 percent said they did not vote because they were not interested in the election or felt their votes would not make a difference.[1]

Of the 32 million people who were not even registered to vote in 2004, 15 million (47 percent) reported that they were not interested in the election or were not involved in politics. Four percent said their votes would not make a difference.[2]

WHEN WE DO VOTE,
OUR VOTES ARE IGNORED

We pride ourselves that our system of government is based on fairness. But fairness is not something that can be determined by the courts or the government. It can be determined only by the people. Is it fair that a single judge can strike down a measure that millions have voted for? In 1994, for instance, 59 percent of the voters in California cast their ballots in favor of Proposition 187, a controversial measure to deny health benefits and education to illegal immigrants. On March 19, 1998, the measure was struck down by a single federal judge, Mariana Pfaelzer, thus denying the voters their prerogative.[3]

ANOTHER SQUEAKER ELECTION

In November 2005, Michael Sessions, an eighteen-year-old high school senior, won the mayoral race in Hillsdale, Michigan (population 9,000), by beating the fifty-one-year-old incumbent 732 to 668.[4] Sessions ran as a write-in candidate because initially he was too young to be placed on the ballot. He used $700 from a summer job to fund his door-to-door campaign. ☆

WHO'S IN CHARGE HERE?

The awful truth is that we the people do not decide the outcome of many elections. The courts do. We don't make the key decisions that affect our lives. The courts do.

Should the Supreme Court, or any court, be able to overrule the will and wishes of millions of Americans? That's a very good question. In case we've forgotten, nine judges, not the people of this country, decided the presidential election of 2000. In one of the closest elections in U.S. history, George W. Bush was declared the winner by a Supreme Court decision that ended the debate about Florida's twenty-five electoral votes.[5] What good is the will of the people if the courts have the ability to overturn our votes and decisions?

What does it tell us when the Supreme Court decides a presidential election? What does it say when millions of Americans vote passionately for a measure, only to have it struck down by a court or a single judge? It tells us very clearly that whether you're a Democrat or a Republican, your vote is often hijacked. Is it right for a few Americans to overturn the wishes of millions of other Americans? Is that fair? Is that democracy?

The simple truth is, if we are not allowed to vote, we do not live in a democracy.

A REPUBLIC, NOT A DEMOCRACY

In school, we are taught that we live in a republic. And in case we forget, the Pledge of Allegiance reminds us of this when we chant, "and to the Republic for which it stands." The dictionary defines a republic as "a country in which the supreme power rests in the body of citizens entitled to vote and is exercised by representatives chosen directly or indirectly by them."[6]

ANOTHER SQUEAKER ELECTION

In 2000, George W. Bush won the presidential election by only 537 votes (some sources say 527). This election was one of the few times in United States history that a candidate won the presidency while losing the nationwide popular vote. The contest hinged on Florida, where that state's twenty-five electoral votes were decided by an official vote count of 537 (or 527) in favor of Bush out of a Florida total of about 6 million votes. In the end, the Supreme Court decided the election, but a few thousand votes one way or another in Florida might have brought a concession speech by one of the contenders and avoided a court-decided victory.[7] ☆

Is a republic different from a democracy? Yes, very different. Here's why: In a democracy, everyone participates. Everyone's vote counts. Instead, we live in a republic, one that many believe has turned into a bureaucracy.

THE ONLY VOICE THAT MATTERS

Politicians pass laws without consulting us, their constituents. They freely spend our money without consulting us. They lead us into wars without our consent. Our political system is set up in this fashion because the country's founders believed that the citizens needed safeguards when making their decisions.

Maybe back in the eighteenth century, this idea made sense. But today, America has a well-educated population. America's citizens are perfectly capable of making their own decisions on matters that affect them. And they should be making those decisions. In the end, we have just one inalienable right: the right to decide our fate for ourselves.

America belongs to us, its citizens. The Constitution is not an antique document but the will and wishes of the people—us. Our voices are the only voices that matter.

With national voting, we would have the final say in the critical issues that face us, such as whether illegal immigration should be tolerated, how our taxes should be spent, and whether drugs should be decriminalized.

Politicians are public servants. They work for us; we do not work for them. If they are not doing their jobs to our satisfaction, it is time for us to do the work for ourselves. As my father used to say, "If you want something done, do it yourself."

2

Americans and Voting
A Love Story

The truth is that Americans love to vote. If the local newspaper asks us to vote on the best steakhouse in town or the best happy-hour appetizers, we eagerly send in our ballots. And we can't resist those online surveys. As I write this, USAToday.com is taking votes on which NBC series should be renewed for another season. Over ten thousand people have voted so far. The *Wall Street Journal*'s OpinionJournal.com site is asking, "Which presidential candidate's biography would you be most likely to read?" So far, more than five thousand people have voted on this burning issue of the day.

But the best proof of what passionate voters we are is *American Idol*. A record 74 million votes were cast in the finale of the 2007 season.[1] That was not only the biggest single voting night in the history of the show, but viewers cast more votes than have ever been cast for a president in a U.S. election. (Ronald Reagan, who got the most votes of any presidential candidate, is a distant second. In 1984 he received 54.5 million votes.)[2]

Now you know something is wrong when more people participate in a talent show than our own political process. But it gets worse. According to a survey reported by ABC News after the 2006 season, not only did nearly one in ten Americans vote during the 2006 season of *American Idol*, but "35 percent of these voters believe their vote to send someone off the *Idol* stage counts at least as much as their vote to send someone to the White House."[3] Many were willing to pay text messaging fees or roaming charges to cast their votes. What does that say about our voting system?

Of course, voting for *American Idol* contestants is easy and convenient. As Ethan J. Leib wrote in the *Washington Post*, "You don't have to get in your car and burn $3-per-gallon gas to get to a polling place; you don't need to wait in line; you don't need to interact with any clumsy bureaucracy or fill out provisional ballots that may or may not get counted. *American Idol* democrats simply pick up the phone or send a text message to vote. No hanging chads here."[4]

What does all this mean? Very simply, we're ready to vote on the important issues, but we can't. The fascinating truth is that the majority of us have already made up our minds on all the issues. We've discussed them over dinner, at work, in the carpool, in line for a movie, and online in chat rooms.

Polls show clearly that the majority of people in this country want something done about illegal immigration, the high cost of gasoline and prescription medications, the wars in Iraq and Afghanistan, and many other issues. But what are our politicians doing to solve these problems? Not much.

WHAT WE'VE GOT NOW

Let's take a moment to briefly review how our system of government operates and consider whether the system in place actually works for us. We vote for politicians who represent us. We give them "power of attorney" so that they can act on our behalf. They, in turn, pass legislation that becomes law. These laws affect our lives and well-being. Yet once we vote candidates into office, how many of us really feel we are consulted or included in this vital decision-making process? Once politicians are elected, the voters who got them their jobs are excluded from the legislative process. The majority's will does not necessarily become law.

ANOTHER SQUEAKER ELECTION

In Virginia, just twenty-four voters could have changed the results of five local elections in November 2005, wrote Calvin R. Trice in the *Richmond Times-Dispatch*. "All those adults with potentially decisive votes could fit comfortably in a school classroom, where one person could give them a civics lesson. In the Jackson River District seat for the Alleghany Board of Supervisors, the difference was a single vote. That race could have been knotted by any registered voter who drove past his precinct by chance, realized it was Election Day, but didn't stop because he figured the lines were too long." Although thousands of votes were cast across the state, races in Alleghany, Charlotte, Clarke, Craig, and Shenandoah counties were won by mere handfuls of votes. Those elections were decided "not by those who didn't show up to vote, but those who did."[5] ☆

We live in a republic, not a democracy. We live in a country ruled not by its people but by its politicians. Any government body that makes decisions on behalf of its people is essentially the ruling body. Over three hundred million Americans are ruled by 9 Supreme Court justices, 100 senators, and 435 congressional representatives.[6] Politicians have ruled over us for more than two centuries. Do you think they've done a good job?

During the late eighteenth century, our country's founders looked around and saw the need to end "taxation without representation." Many of us today see "Congress without representation." In other words, the representatives we send to Congress seem, at some point, to stop representing us and start representing the lobbyists and special interests. Many people feel the lobbyists and special interests are the ones who are pulling the lever in Washington. They are calling the shots, and they have too much power. According to the Center for Public Integrity, "more than 22,000 companies and organizations have employed 3,500 lobbying firms and more than 27,000 lobbyists since 1998."[7] That's a lot of influence.

Is this what our nation's founders had in mind? They wanted the people to decide, not lobbyists.

Even politicians are often excluded from direct action because much in Congress is determined by committees and subcommittees. Do you know that the Senate and the House of Representatives combined have over two hundred committees and subcommittees?[8] They hold hearings on just about anything, all at great taxpayer expense. No wonder very little gets done.

The result is that our problems are left alone until they become crises. When Hurricane Katrina devastated the population of New Orleans and surrounding areas, it became painfully clear that the Federal Emergency Management Agency (FEMA) was not functioning the way it needed to. The Army Corps of Engineers had been asking for money for at least a decade to shore up the levee system surrounding New Orleans. The levee system failed and the result was devastating flooding. By most estimates, rebuilding New Orleans will cost taxpayers more than $200 billion.[9] The Army Corps of Engineers was asking for $27 million.[10]

NATIONAL VOTING AND OUR COUNTRY'S FOUNDERS

In the Declaration of Independence, our country's founders said, "All men are created equal." Voting gives us that equality, but only if our votes matter and only if we vote. Is the system we have now really what our nation's founders wanted for this country? Is it unpatriotic to want your country to work better?

Our country's founders feared they would be hanged for treason if they signed the Declaration of Independence. But they signed anyway. Later on, Jefferson himself expressed doubts about the Constitution, but he believed it was better to put something in motion rather than do nothing at all. (And remember that the Constitution was written because the original plan, the Articles of Confederation, didn't work.) The truth is that like our nation's founders, we won't know what works until we try it.

If those who helped craft the Constitution were alive and serving in our government today, they would find their ideas bogged down in subcommittees, rewritten by lobbyists, and defeated by special interests. They would find that the political system they invented was polarized and entangled in gridlock. On the other hand, they would have special license plates so they could park anywhere in Washington, cushy offices, pensions for life (even if they had to resign in disgrace), and the best healthcare plan in the country.

WHAT'S THE SOLUTION?

Too many people—politicians, lobbyists, judges, and more—stand between us and the decisions that need to be made. No wonder we don't bother to vote. Declining voter participation is a serious threat to the health of our democracy, wrote Phil Keisling, former Oregon secretary of state. "Midterm elections are now attracting just 35–40 percent participation. Far, far worse are primary elections . . . For these contests, turnout has been truly abysmal—in many states 5 to 15 percent of the eligible population."[11]

ANOTHER SQUEAKER ELECTION

In 1839, Marcus "Landslide" Morton was elected governor of Massachusetts by one vote. He received 51,034 of the 102,066 votes cast. Had the vote been tied at 51,033, the election would have been decided in the legislature, which would probably have chosen his opponent. Amazingly, in 1842, Landslide did it again, winning the same office by one vote in the legislature.[12] ☆

The solution to this lack of voting is more voting. Yes, you read that right. National voting can be a tool to ignite the passion that is in all Americans but that's become dormant. National voting would allow our voices to be heard and to count because national voting is one person, one vote.

Andy Rooney gets it. In a *60 Minutes* piece called "Let's Vote . . . on Everything," he said, "We don't vote on every issue. Our elected officials do that for us. We don't always agree with them, of course . . . Maybe we don't vote often enough."[13]

With national voting, we'd all have plenty of chances to vote. Maybe not as many as *American Idol* offers, but we'd be voting on the issues that matter.

3

Thinking Outside the Ballot Box

Every movement in this country—the American Revolution, the abolition of slavery, women's right to vote, the civil rights movement—began with a simple idea. Every constitutional amendment got its start when some people questioned the status quo and decided a change was needed. Americans have never been afraid to try something new. Thomas Jefferson, Thomas Payne, and Martin Luther King Jr. all had ideas to make this country better, and they weren't afraid to take action.

WHAT IS NATIONAL VOTING?

National voting is also known as *direct democracy*. It's a political system that can be traced back to ancient Athens. The Romans also practiced it. In a direct democracy, the power belongs not to the politicians but to the people.

The Swiss practice a form of direct democracy. Between 1892 and 2004, Swiss citizens put more than 240 initiatives to public referendum. The populace has been conservative, approving only 14 percent of the initiatives put before it; in addition, it has often opted for versions of initiatives rewritten by government personnel.[1]

Many communities in New England use direct democracy to decide local issues. Their town hall meetings are a well-known example of citizens deciding for themselves how to run their communities.

At the state and local levels, various kinds of direct democracy are common. In more than half the states and in numerous localities, citizens are directly involved in making, changing, or repealing laws. Measures proposed by citizens (initiatives) or by the legislature are submitted to a popular vote by referendum.[3] In eighteen states citizens also have the power to remove public officials from office, using a process known as recall. The removal of California governor Gray Davis from office in 2003 is a well-known example of a recall election. The recall process does not exist at the federal level, however.

THE POWER OF DIRECT DEMOCRACY

Many of our current issues—gun control, health insurance, abortion—could be decided with a national vote. Here's one way the general process could work:

1. American citizens would identify the issues and then put them to a vote. A national citizens' committee would draft the language for the ballot.
2. We would register our preferences by going to the polls, mailing in our ballots, phoning in our votes, or voting online.
3. The ballot items with a majority vote would immediately become law and would remain law for ten years.

It's that simple.

After an election, no court or legal challenge of any kind would be allowed. No single judge or group of judges could rule a vote unconstitutional because in this new system, everything would be up for grabs. For instance, if the people voted to ban guns nationwide (except for the military and law enforcement), the Second Amendment of the Constitution would have to be repealed.

People could protest all they wanted, but once the votes were tallied, the decision would be final and we would all live with the results for a decade. After a decade, the issue could be put on the table again.

This system would put an end to the nonstop debating and bickering that often paralyzes our lawmakers. It would make voting citizens—not politicians—the decision makers and the lawmakers. Once the people had spoken, their say would be final. Congress would take our decisions and formulate the statutes needed to implement them. For example, if we voted to outlaw tobacco, Congress would draft the legislation necessary to make all tobacco products illegal, to enforce penalties for those who violate the laws, and to end the growing of tobacco and the production of tobacco products.

Of course, voters would need to consider the cost of the programs they vote on, but this would come in subsequent votes on an issue. For instance, the first vote on illegal immigration would determine whether it will be tolerated or not. If the voters decide it should not be tolerated, later votes would determine how much should be spent to reinforce our borders and so on.

Congress could still debate and work out the details, but hot topics that need clarification—school prayer, medical marijuana, and immigration, to name a few—should be put to a citizens' vote.

WHY NOT?

Would national voting lead to a mob mentality where the majority group rules, leaving no option for minority rights? This is a commonly heard argument against any form of direct democracy. The answer is no. For starters, national voting wouldn't create anarchy because the people would make very specific rules about how the system would work. For instance, strict guidelines would be created to regulate how much each side could spend on its campaign.

The system would be very different from what we have now. But *different* doesn't necessarily mean *anarchy*. The kinds of direct democracy already being practiced—initiatives, referendums, and town hall meetings, for example—do not lead to anarchy. The California recall election in 2003 may have seemed chaotic at times because of the wide assortment of people who decided to run for governor, but the election was orderly and fair.

Many people will argue that national voting is unworkable because, outside of Switzerland, it has never been tested on a national scale. It's true that the United States is much bigger than Switzerland. But if the producers of *American Idol* can collect and count votes from tens of millions of people, week after week, is there any doubt that the United States of America, with all its technological resources, can find a way to make national voting a simple, workable, fair process?

And remember the definition of *insanity*: doing the same thing over and over again and expecting different results. We keep electing politicians who don't look after the public's will. They're too busy stuffing bills with costly pork that will benefit special interests. If Louisiana needs an infusion of aid after Hurricane Katrina, money should be appropriated for that purpose only, not earmarked for additional uses that have nothing to do with hurricane relief.

Is "business as usual" in our political government better than a system untried? Politicians are keenly aware that public opinion is sovereign in this country. Journalists believe they are taking the temperature of the American public by conducting endless polls. But polling is not voting. When it comes to action, public opinion doesn't count for much. On innumerable occasions, judges and politicians have completely disregarded our wishes.

THE NAYSAYERS

When I speak to groups or give interviews about national voting, I am often astonished at the reactions some people have.

The very groups that I expected to be the most open-minded and willing to embrace the idea of a national vote have been the most defensive about our present, broken system. They would rather not discuss other possibilities. They believe that the only way to change the political process in Washington is to launch massive letter-writing campaigns to our elected officials, making them aware of our discontent.

At the Democratic Club of West Orange County (California), one man at the back of the room said that state laws for the most part remain intact. I said, "That may be true, but they are still vulnerable to rulings by the Supreme Court." I mentioned the medical marijuana law in California. This initiative, Proposition 215, was passed by the people of California on November 5, 1996. It is a state law now, the Compassionate Use Act of 1996.[4] But because federal agents can (and will) ar-

ANOTHER SQUEAKER ELECTION

In Orange County, California, Janet Nguyen was elected to the county board of supervisors by just three votes. She took office on March 26, 2007, forty-nine days after a special election held on February 6. On election night she was ahead by fifty-two votes, but late ballots gave the victory to her opponent, Trung Nguyen, the leader by just seven votes. She requested a recount and won the election by seven votes, four of which were later overturned.[5] ☆

rest vendors under federal narcotics laws, the state law that was passed doesn't mean anything.

Another man said, "Well, we'll just change the federal law."

People such as this man are passionate about the system we have right now—even though it doesn't work. They know it's broken, but they are waiting for the politicians to reform themselves. That's like asking the fox to guard the henhouse.

It's understandable that some people would rather stick with something familiar than try something new and unknown. The trick is to convince them that cosmetic reforms are not going to work and that we need to try something completely new.

Others are so discouraged by our present system that they have given up hope. I spoke to two men who called the *Help Me Rhonda Show* on KDAL-AM (Duluth, Minnesota). Both were very pessimistic. They believe we can't do anything to change our government.

As Rhonda Grussendorf, the host, said, "A terrible wave of apathy has gripped this nation to the point where people see that any positive change is impossible."[6]

WHAT HAVE WE GOT TO LOSE?

What would we gain by national voting? National voting would make us think and it would make us act. It would level the playing field. National voting would be the great equalizer because everyone's vote would be equal. It would cut out special interests. It would protect measures we vote on by ensuring that they will become law for ten years. It would finally resolve controversial issues fairly and, as a result, create tremendous peace of mind. We would finally see the big problems that face our country actually getting solved.

4

We've Got the Smarts to Do It Ourselves

Don't you think Americans are smart enough to decide the great issues of the day? America is the nation that put men on the moon, that helped join the entire world into a global family through the personal computer and the Internet, that created great agricultural productivity and advances in medical science. It's a nation that combines common sense, visionary thinking, and the will and determination to accomplish what we set out to do.

Aren't we smart enough to figure out a path for our country, to know how to move forward past the endless debates about abortion, gun control, free speech, universal healthcare, terrorism, taxation, immigration, and the national debt and find workable solutions for these problems? And aren't we smart enough to design a system, most likely one that uses our current technology, to make our wishes a reality?

We have been conditioned to believe that we have very little recourse against our government, that it's something we're stuck with. But Thomas Jefferson wrote in the Declaration of Independence, "That whenever any Form of Government becomes destructive of these ends, it is the Right of the People to alter or to abolish it, and to institute new Government."

Translated, that says that if a government or a certain type of government is no longer working for us, it is our duty to change it.

Does taking the power back and making decisions for ourselves seem like an impossibility? How many people thought the same about America's independence from Britain, the abolition of slavery, or the civil rights movement? When an idea is right, Americans can come together and make it a reality.

ANOTHER SQUEAKER ELECTION

In the November 2005 election, Randy Farkas, a Republican, was declared the winner in a race for a borough council seat in Milltown, New Jersey, by one vote over his Democratic opponent, Joseph Cruz. "It is a great civics lesson," Farkas told a reporter right after election night when the tally stood at 1,363 to 1,362. "It's just one of those other things that we take for granted; one vote really does matter."[1] Eight days later, after twenty absentee ballots were counted, the vote shifted toward Cruz, making him the official winner, 1,369 to 1,368. Cruz called his victory "bittersweet."

"Who wants to win an election like that?" he told a reporter from the local paper. "Election season is tough enough. This made it even tougher."[2] ☆

THE NUTS AND BOLTS
OF NATIONAL VOTING

In national voting, everyone would get to vote, much like the popular vote in presidential elections, except in national voting the popular vote would count. Here are the basics of national voting.

- Just as now, you would have to be a citizen and at least eighteen to vote.
- Elections would be held four times a year, on March 1, June 1, September 1, and December 1.
- At each quarterly election, ten measures would be voted on. How would these measures be chosen? We the people would do that too.
- Prior to each voting date, people could suggest issues to vote on. These ideas, complaints, and gripes would be sent by e-mail, mail, fax, and phone to a giant national call center.
- The ten measures that received the most suggestions would be voted on during the next quarterly election. From time to time, an emergency or other urgent issue might arise (such as a war or a national disaster) and a special election would be scheduled.
- Only one suggestion per subject would be allowed per person, so every idea would have to be accompanied by a name, address, phone number, and some kind of identification number. We might decide to use a person's driver's license or Social Security number for verification. Or we might give every voter a special voter identification number to use for this purpose.

An e-mail suggestion form might look like this:

Subject:

Brief description:

Name:

Address:

Phone number:

Identification number (password or PIN):

Once the issues were chosen, here's how the election would work:

- Two weeks before the election, ballots would be mailed to all voters.
- Voters would research the issues, make their decisions, and cast their ballots by phone, by e-mail, or at their local polling place.
- Ballots would be tallied by the individual states.
- The results would be sent to the Government Accountability Office in Washington, DC, for the final tally.
- The outcome of the vote would become law for ten years. Ten years is long enough to see if a law works but short enough to make changes if they're necessary.
- All laws passed by the people would be up for renewal after a decade.

NATIONAL VOTING IN ACTION

Are you still not sure what national voting would be like? Let's imagine Katie and Sam Driscoll and watch as they vote on the issue of tax reform.

Sydney Nixon took his seat as a Vermont state representative in 1977, having apparently won the election, 570 to 569. However, a recount determined that he had in fact lost to Robert Emond, 572 to 571, and Nixon resigned.[3] ☆

Katie is twenty-seven and Sam is thirty. He's an auto mechanic who makes good money. They have two children, ages three and five. Katie is an office manager in a busy doctor's office. They are two average, hard-working, healthy Americans. But despite their two incomes, they never have enough money. They would like to buy a house someday and maybe have another baby, but they can't seem to save a dime. They look at their pay stubs and realize they are being taxed out of the lifestyle they dream of. They strongly believe that the American tax system needs reforming.

So Katie sends an e-mail to the National Voting Call Center. She puts "Tax reform" in the subject line and writes this brief description: "Our tax system is unfair and much too complicated. Our taxes are too high. We need tax reform." Then she adds her name, address, telephone number, and driver's license number. Sam sends a text message with a similar suggestion to the call center during a brief break at work.

And they aren't alone. Over 57 million Americans suggest this issue, and their voices are heard. Measure 251: Tax Reform becomes a National Voting Measure on the March 1 ballot.

Two weeks before March 1, the ballots are mailed and voting begins. This gives people enough time to mail in their ballots. The system is so user friendly that people have actually started to vote again, and they vote in huge numbers—numbers usually reserved for *American Idol* participants.

With their busy schedules, Katie and Sam appreciate the full two weeks they have to make their decisions. They stay up late and research their measure and the other nine issues online. There's a lot of debate about the election on television, on the radio, and in blogs and print media, too. Katie and Sam really take their time to think about everything they're voting on. After all, the results of this vote will become law for ten years. And with national voting, every vote makes a difference.

They are more careful now than they used to be when they voted—well, when Katie voted. Sam stopped voting after the 2000 election when the Supreme Court, not the citizens, elected the president. But since national voting began, he hasn't missed an election.

On March 1, they get up early. After making coffee, they each check their e-mail and the day's news online. Then they take turns logging on with their personal security codes and voting.

Sam's parents are older and less comfortable with the idea of online voting, so they phone their votes in. Phone votes are handled by the same security system used for online voting. It was developed when national voting was first passed. Some people still vote in local polling places. But most voters prefer to vote from home, the way we do so much else in the twenty-first century: banking online, shopping from home, working from home, taking classes from home, and now voting from home.

After the election, the Government Accountability Office tabulates the votes, and the results are released a week later. Tax Reform passes by a very wide margin. Overjoyed, Katie and Sam celebrate, taking their children and Sam's parents out to dinner as a special treat. Thanks to the tax reform measure that is now the law, they hope to be able to afford dinner out more often.

5

What Would Change— and What Wouldn't

If we lived in a real democracy, we would be able to find solutions ourselves for our country's problems, the issues that directly affect our lives. If we lived in a country where every vote mattered, we would finally see results. We would be able to decide issues such as abortion and gun control, and our decisions would last for at least a decade. We would have a say in how taxes are raised and how they are spent. We would be able to find creative ways other than income taxes to fill the government coffers. Our government would not be just for the people but truly by the people.

THE NEW PRESIDENT

But what would happen to the government we have now? It wouldn't go away. With national voting, the president would not be president of the United States but president *for* the United States. In the past, people have looked to their presidents to solve their problems. Now the people themselves would be the problem solvers. The new president would simply be the chief administrator of the people's wishes. He or she would follow our orders and make sure our wishes were carried out. No longer would a president have the power to veto the will of the people or to lead us into wars without our consent. Never again would a president wield as much power as recent presidents have wielded.

THE NEW CONGRESS AND SUPREME COURT

Instead of counting on a representative to do it for us, with national voting we would vote on measures directly. The people would make the laws, change the laws, and rewrite their Constitution. Laws would be drawn very clearly so as to leave no room for interpretation.

Under national voting our elected representatives would still have a role to play. First, they would continue to represent us. They would be our faithful watchdogs, guarding our votes and making sure they are carried out. When the people voted on an issue and it became law, our representatives would constantly be on the lookout for anyone or any group that tried to reverse or subvert that vote. They would make sure that such people were prosecuted. Second, they would handle legislation such as highway and energy bills, making sure the flow of electricity was uninterrupted during heat waves and natural disasters.

The Supreme Court would have a part to play as well. The Court would rule only on issues and cases the people have not already decided on. The people would tell the Court what cases to hear, instead of the other way around. In other words, the Supreme Court's docket would be based on the issues the people wanted the Court to hear. For instance, if the people did not want to resolve the issue of illegal immigration themselves, they would turn this over to the Court to be resolved. However, the Supreme Court would not be able to hear cases on any issues that the people had already decided with a national vote.

The lower courts would remain a fundamental part of our judicial system because they would raise issues for the people (or the Supreme Court) to resolve. People would still be able to initiate court cases that do not present constitutional challenges to the laws they have voted on.

Supreme Court justices keep their positions for life. Therefore, it is vitally important that the people of this nation nominate and elect their justices. Another alternative the people might want to consider is electing new justices every decade so that the Court better reflects the wishes of the people at any given time. In either case, the members of the Supreme Court would honor our wishes and make sure the laws we pass are protected.

In June 2005, for instance, the U.S. Supreme Court had a chance to strengthen the legal protection for victims of domestic violence. Instead, the Court declined, ruling that law enforcement officers were not obliged to enforce restraining orders in all circumstances.[1] This is an issue people need to vote on directly. It's too important to be left to the Court.

PAPER OR ELECTRONIC?

The way we vote has been quietly changing for a long time. In Oregon, all voting is now done by mail. Absentee voting, another way of voting by mail, is increasingly common. Nearly half of California voters cast absentee ballots, and in Washington, nearly 70 percent. According to early estimates, one in four ballots in the 2006 election was cast before election day.[2]

Technology has brought new ways to vote and new problems with our electoral system. In many parts of the country, voting machines have caused confusion, long delays, and much, much worse. At times the system doesn't work at all:

when registered voters are denied the right to vote, when machines don't properly count the ballots, or when paperless voting records can't be audited but can be manipulated.

An analysis at Princeton of the hardware and software of the Diebold AccuVote-TS paperless voting machine showed it was "vulnerable to extremely serious attacks." Someone could remove the machine's memory card and in one minute install malicious code that could "steal votes undetectably, modifying all records, logs, and counters to be consistent with the fraudulent vote count it creates." An attacker could also create "a voting-machine virus" that would spread "automatically and silently from machine to machine during normal election activities."[4]

In 2006, Robin Williams starred in a black comedy, *Man of the Year*, that addressed this scandal. Williams played a talk show host who was accidentally elected president as a result of a glitch in the voting-machine program.

If we're going to be voting every quarter, we need to solve these problems. But a country where people safely and securely shop and bank online every day should be able to develop safeguards that will protect our votes.

PROTECTING OUR VOTES

Voting is precious in our country and should be protected. What safeguards should be in place to protect the voting rights of citizens, not from badly designed voting machines but from people who want to usurp our power? What kind of punishments should there be for those who interfere with our wishes?

We need to create strict laws with heavy fines and mandatory prison sentences to protect our votes and punish those who violate or interfere with the voting process or who try to overturn the votes. Those who are disloyal to their country or who betray its trust can be considered traitors. The people

---

ANOTHER SQUEAKER ELECTION

In South Dakota in 1997, the race for the second seat in Legislative District 12 was another close one. On election night, John McIntyre had 4,195 votes to Hal Wick's 4,191. However, a recount showed Wick was the winner, 4,192 votes to 4,191. When the state supreme court ruled that an overvote made one ballot cast for Wick invalid, the race was a tie. Finally, the state legislature voted 46–20 to give the election to Wick.[5] ☆

---

may decide that those who go against their will or who interfere with their decisions are also betraying their country and should be considered traitors as well. And treason is a very serious offense.

Under national voting, voter fraud, vote tampering, or attempting to overturn a law the people have passed—with a court challenge or a legal complaint—would be severely punished. Civil servants, federal employees, federal judges, and members of the military would have to abide by even stricter rules because they have sworn to serve us.

Protesting over issues or the outcome of national voting would always be permissible. Attempting to overturn votes that are made into laws by the people would not.

CONCLUSION

National voting is not a political party. It is a political movement. Even better, it's a nonpartisan movement. That's good for this country—we don't need any more divisiveness in America today. We need ideas that can unite us and make us strong, not divide us and weaken us.

National voting is not about reforming either the political parties or the politicians. It is about trying something completely new.

Thomas Jefferson said, "a little rebellion now and then is a good thing . . . It is a medicine necessary for the sound health of government."[6] He believed we should revisit the Constitution every twenty years. We're way behind schedule.

We the people needs to mean something again, and with national voting it can. We need a voice in what happens in our country. Let's get moving!

PART TWO

The Issues

Make Your Voice Heard

The time for talking and arguing is over. Now you must vote on the issues yourself. For the first time in American history, you will be in charge of your own destiny. If you don't vote, your voice will not be heard. It's time to untie the legal and congressional knot that has a stranglehold on our nation. The decisions that affect our lives and our futures are too important to be left in the hands of politicians or the courts. Only we can speak for ourselves.

In this section, you'll find the most significant and controversial issues facing American citizens today. To make sure that you find issues you care deeply about, this first round of national voting offers thirty-one issues instead of ten. I've grouped them by topic so you can see how national voting can be applied to a wide variety of our country's problems. Each issue is described, and the arguments for and against are summarized. Record your own opinion under the heading "Choose One."

Many of these issues are ones you already have a strong opinion about. Some may be new issues to you. Like Katie and Sam Driscoll in chapter 4, you'll probably need to do some research. You'll find some useful resources in the appendix. Or you can start with a search for the issue at Google News or another news site. Libraries have free databases of newspaper and magazine articles, such as ProQuest, EBSCOhost, and NewsBank. If you have a library card, you can often access these resources remotely and study the issues at home, in your neighborhood coffeehouse, or wherever it's convenient.

I suggest you make your choices in pencil first in case you change your mind. Once you've made your choices, record them in ink on the perforated ballot at the back of the book or at the end of part 2. You can photocopy the ballot so more than one person in your household can vote. After you've finished voting, write your name and address on the ballot, put a first-class stamp on it, and mail it to

The President of the United States of America
The White House
1600 Pennsylvania Avenue NW
Washington, DC 20500

By doing this you are demanding that your president send your ballot to the Government Accountability Office to be counted with others like it. You're also demanding that once the votes are tabulated and confirmed, they become law for ten years.

Remember that we elected the president and, like it or not, he or she has to listen to us and take action to make sure our wishes become law.

Constitutional Amendments

The Constitution of the United States of America guarantees us certain rights and liberties. Since it was written, it has been amended twenty-seven times, including the first ten amendments, called the Bill of Rights.

FOR

The Constitution is not an antique document but a sacred expression of the wishes and will of the American people. At issue here is whether the thoughts and philosophies generated in eighteenth-century America are still relevant. Thomas Jefferson, the architect of the Constitution, was acutely aware of the need to reevaluate the underpinnings of the country. He suggested that the Constitution be revisited every twenty years.

AGAINST

The Constitution is a sacred document that in no way should be tampered with. It has protected us since the founding of the country and has enough flexibility built into it to continue working even if it is never changed. Changing interpretations of the material in the Constitution keep it alive and well.

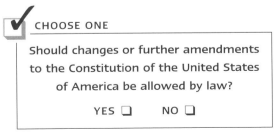

CHOOSE ONE

Should changes or further amendments to the Constitution of the United States of America be allowed by law?

YES ❑   NO ❑

Democracy

In a democracy, everyone participates. Everyone's vote counts. In a democracy, power is vested in the people and they make the decisions for themselves. America is a republic. A republic is a country in which people turn their power over to their elected representatives, who make the decisions for them.

FOR

Being a republic is not working for us any longer. Our government has turned into a bureaucracy. The Declaration of Independence says, "That whenever any Form of Government becomes destructive of these ends, it is the Right of the People to alter or to abolish it, and to institute new Government." This means that if a government or a certain type of government is no longer working for us, it is our duty to change it.

AGAINST

Our system of government functions well. Direct democracy breeds anarchy and mob rule. Our current political system is far from perfect, but it provides the necessary checks and balances needed to keep civil law and order and maintain the status quo. It keeps our country from descending into chaos.

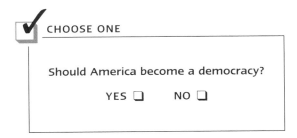

CHOOSE ONE

Should America become a democracy?

YES ☐   NO ☐

The Electoral College

American voters do not vote directly for the president and vice president. When they mark their ballots for a particular candidate, they are actually choosing a slate of members of the Electoral College. These electors then vote for the president and vice president. A total of 538 electors are divided among the states. Each state has one elector for each of its U.S. representatives plus one for each of its U.S. senators. The candidate who wins the most votes in a particular state "carries the state"; that is, he or she wins all the electors of that state. Thus, a candidate can have more votes nationwide but still lose the election in the Electoral College.[1]

FOR

The Electoral College system was established by the Constitution, and this method of tabulating votes in a presidential election works. This voting method has run smoothly for more than two hundred years; any other system would be cumbersome and potentially unfair.

AGAINST

Voting is our most sacred right; every individual vote should count. The majority of the people who cast their ballots on November 7, 2000, cast them in favor of one man, who won the popular vote by just under 400,000 votes but who lost the election because he had fewer electoral votes. That election was not decided by the people of this country but by five justices of the Supreme Court who voted along party lines. The

2000 election demonstrated that the votes of the people of this nation do not count. The Electoral College has got to go.

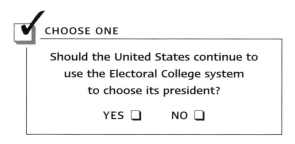

CHOOSE ONE

Should the United States continue to use the Electoral College system to choose its president?

YES ❏   NO ❏

Pensions for Politicians and Federal Employees

Federal workers and elected politicians are guaranteed lifetime pensions by law. Since January 2007, federal employees can lose their pensions if they are convicted of certain crimes, including bribery, conspiracy, perjury, treason, and espionage.[2] But officials who are forced to resign in disgrace still keep their lifetime pensions.

FOR

Federal employees and elected officials should receive lifetime pensions because they work hard for us and deserve to be rewarded for their service. In addition, these pensions have been promised, and canceling them would be unfair to federal workers who are counting on that income for retirement.

AGAINST

Corporate pensions are disappearing. In the post-Enron era, working Americans are more vulnerable than ever before. Despite decades of work for a company, their pensions are at risk. American workers are exasperated to think they can lose their corporate pensions because of incompetence or mismanagement by CEOs while the federal government, which has set new milestones in incompetence, rewards federal workers and politicians for their poor performance. Our country can find better ways to spend this money.

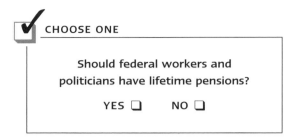

CHOOSE ONE

Should federal workers and
politicians have lifetime pensions?

YES ☐   NO ☐

Affirmative Action

Affirmative action generally means giving preferential treatment to minorities in admission to universities or employment in government and businesses. Affirmative action policies were originally developed to correct decades of discrimination and to give disadvantaged minorities a boost. The diversity of our current society compared with that of fifty years ago seems to indicate that such programs have been a success.

FOR

All people should be treated equally and fairly. Diversity is desirable and won't always occur if left to chance. Affirmative action draws people to areas of work they might never consider otherwise. Some stereotypes may never be broken without affirmative action. Affirmative action is needed to compensate minorities for centuries of slavery or oppression.

AGAINST

No segment of the population should be singled out for special treatment based on race or ethnicity. An individual should be appointed to a position based on his or her qualifications. Affirmative action leads to reverse discrimination. Affirmative action lowers the standards of accountability needed to push students or employees to perform better. To imply that they need affirmative action to succeed is condescending to minorities. When success seems to result from affirmative action rather than hard work and ability, true minority achievement is demeaned.

CHOOSE ONE

Should affirmative action policies,
which give preferential treatment
based on minority status, be protected?

YES ❑   NO ❑

Eminent Domain

Eminent domain is the power of a government to force private landowners to sell their property for "public use." Previously, eminent domain has been used for public purposes such as highways and bridges, public parks, schools, government facilities, and municipal buildings. Also, local governments have used eminent domain to take over "blighted" property and redevelop it. In June 2005, however, the United States Supreme Court ruled that private property could be seized and sold for private development when it would benefit the public by increasing tax revenues.[3]

FOR

Eminent domain for private economic development is a useful tool to help cities revitalize rundown urban neighborhoods. For example, in the Northeast, the supply of suburban land is dwindling and many city centers have fallen into decay.

AGAINST

Forcibly shifting land from one private owner to another, even with fair compensation, violates the Fifth Amendment to the Constitution. The amendment clearly prohibits the taking of property by government except for "public use." In addition, elderly, minority, and low-income urban residents are likely to be displaced from their homes.

CHOOSE ONE

Should private property be forcibly
taken and sold for the use of
private urban development?

YES ❏   NO ❏

Free Speech

The First Amendment to the Constitution guarantees us the rights of free speech and free expression. It does not, however, allow reckless behavior. We are not free to shout "fire" in a crowded theater when there is no threat or to shout "bomb" on a commercial airliner.

FOR

Free speech is an essential ingredient of American life. It is part of our history. The Constitution automatically guarantees us our freedom of expression.

AGAINST

Much of the moral decay that has occurred in our country can be directly blamed on violent films and videos and pornography that are protected under the guise of free speech and free expression. As a first measure in protecting our children, freedom of speech and expression should be curtailed.

CHOOSE ONE

Should freedom of speech
always be protected?

YES ❏   NO ❏

Mandatory National Service

Mandatory national service, also known as a draft, would direct all young men and women between the ages of eighteen and twenty-six to serve two years in a branch of the armed forces.

FOR

Mandatory national service is an effective way to secure the numbers we need in the armed forces to protect our country.

AGAINST

A volunteer army of trained professional soldiers is better suited for combat than a drafted one. The draft didn't work in the Vietnam era, and it won't work now.

CHOOSE ONE

Should national service be mandatory?

YES ☐   NO ☐

National Identity Card

A national identity card would identify U.S. citizens as Americans. It would be similar to a passport, but passports are intended only for travel outside the United States. A national identity card could not be used outside the country. The card would simply verify a person's identity.

FOR

Billions of dollars of taxpayers' money are being spent on medical care and education for illegal immigrants. A national identity card would help to identify citizens and others who are here legally at the time of medical treatment, employment, or school enrollment. Apart from our passports, we have no documentation to distinguish us as Americans. Most Americans do not have U.S. passports, and those who do are rarely asked to produce them inside the country for the purpose of identification.

AGAINST

Requiring a national identity card would violate our civil rights and our right to privacy. It would also be a complete waste of time because, like a lot of other official documents, a national identity card could easily be forged.

CHOOSE ONE

Should every American citizen be required
to have a national identity card?

YES ❏   NO ❏

National Language

A national language is a single language used for all of a country's official communication.

FOR

We live in America, and in this country we speak English. Using one language, and one language only, would ease the congestion created by two or more languages being spoken in many businesses and branches of government.

Millions of dollars could be saved annually in this country if a national language were instituted. Ballots, driving tests and manuals, and countless other state and federal publications are currently printed in several languages, all at great taxpayer expense. If people become naturalized citizens of the United States of America, they need to learn to speak, read, and write English so as not to burden the system with multiple languages.

AGAINST

Although a single national language would be a good idea, it is too late to turn back the clock. Most businesses and government agencies are already equipped to accommodate customers who speak Spanish or other languages besides English.

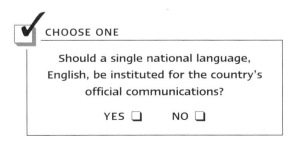

CHOOSE ONE

Should a single national language, English, be instituted for the country's official communications?

YES ☐   NO ☐

Alcohol and Tobacco Prohibition

Alcohol and tobacco are drugs that have been enjoyed in our country for centuries. They are both currently legal, but their use is regulated and taxed. For example, smokers can't light up wherever they want to, underage people cannot legally buy these products, and we pay federal and state taxes when we purchase tobacco products or alcohol.

FOR

Prohibiting alcohol and tobacco use would save hundreds of lives each year in our country. Alcohol is to blame for more than 17,000 deaths on American roads annually, according to statistics compiled by the National Highway Traffic Safety Administration (NHTSA) and reported on the Mothers Against Drunk Driving Web site.[4] Of the 6,409 traffic fatalities in 2003 involving young people between the ages of fifteen and twenty, 2,283 were alcohol related.[5] With teenagers having easy access to liquor, alcoholism begins early in our society.

Tobacco, nicknamed "the killer weed," is directly responsible for nearly half a million deaths a year in the United States.[6] Our taxes subsidize tobacco farmers, and these subsidies should end.

AGAINST

Prohibition in the 1920s did nothing to curb alcohol intake. In fact, it had the opposite effect. It sent America on one of the biggest drinking binges it has ever known. It also spawned organized crime and made those who trafficked in illegal alcohol incredibly wealthy. It is an adult's prerogative to decide whether to consume legal drugs. Millions of Americans enjoy tobacco and alcohol; legislating lifestyle and morality is a waste of time and a poor use of taxpayers' money.

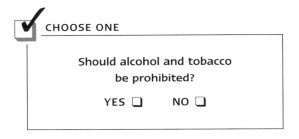

CHOOSE ONE

**Should alcohol and tobacco
be prohibited?**

YES ☐   NO ☐

Narcotics
Decriminalization

Narcotics such as cocaine, marijuana, and heroin are illegal in this country. Decriminalizing these substances would mean their use would no longer be a crime. However, use of narcotics would probably still be regulated, just as alcohol use and tobacco use are.

FOR

Taking drugs is a personal choice, no different from smoking cigarettes or drinking alcohol. In addition, prohibition is a losing battle; we need look no further than the failure of alcohol prohibition during the 1920s in our country to see how a law meant to do good did harm instead.

Toleration is a much better approach. Consider the Dutch model, which has yielded positive results in the war against drugs. Holland tolerates all the substances that we don't, yet it does not have the level of crime we have. Federal and state governments in the United States spend more than $40 billion a year on the war against drugs. That money would be better spent on education and drug treatment.[7]

AGAINST

Illegal narcotics are the cause of thousands of deaths each year in this country. If made legal, their use would increase and the number of overdoses would rise. Also, the drugs would find their way into the hands of children much more readily. People need to be protected from themselves.

✓ CHOOSE ONE

Should narcotics be decriminalized?

YES ❑   NO ❑

Pornography

Pornography is any sexually explicit writing and/or picture intended to arouse sexual desire.

FOR

Pornography is a form of expression that is protected under the First Amendment. It's enjoyed by millions of adults in this country. Clearly people want it. The statistics are staggering: 4.2 million Web sites are devoted to pornographic content, and it's estimated that about two hundred new sex-related Web sites are added every day.[8] Parents must take responsibility to monitor their children's viewing habits to ensure that they are not exposed to pornography, but adults should be able to have access to it if they wish.

AGAINST

Pornography has no place in our lives. It may be a multibillion-dollar business, but it has no place in the economy of this country. It's demeaning to women, and it has the potential to corrupt our children or, worse, cause them genuine harm. Pornography is an ever-growing threat and needs to be stamped out.

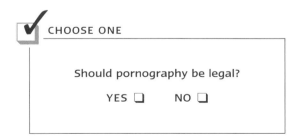

CHOOSE ONE

Should pornography be legal?

YES ❏   NO ❏

Prostitution

Prostitution is the performance of sexual acts for money.

FOR

Prostitution is the "world's oldest profession" for a reason, and it is unlikely that any individual or government will ever successfully stamp it out. Legislating a consensual sexual transaction between adults is virtually impossible.

Prior to the early twentieth century, prostitution was tolerated nationwide. Today's rise in the crime rate is due not only to drug prohibition but also to the banning of prostitution. Holland provides a good example of how to handle prostitution. The Dutch government turned it into a business and a tourist attraction by legalizing it for anyone eighteen or older who acts freely, not under coercion.[9] In countries such as Holland that tolerate prostitution, the law recognizes the impossibility of legislating sex. Like pornography, prostitution is a pastime enjoyed by tens of thousands of Americans, despite the fact that it is illegal in most of the country. A 2004 survey conducted by TNS, a research company, found that three out of ten single men age thirty and over have paid for sex.[10]

AGAINST

Like pornography, prostitution has no place in our society. And like pornography, it has the potential to corrupt our children. Prostitution is an eyesore that pollutes entire neighborhoods.

Should prostitution be legal?

YES ❏   NO ❏

Same-Sex Marriage

Traditionally, marriage has been a union between a man and a woman.

FOR

Current laws unfairly discriminate against gays and lesbians. Same-sex couples should be entitled to the same rights and privileges as any other couples.

AGAINST

Marriage, especially as defined in the Bible, can only be between a man and a woman. Domestic partnerships offer plenty of rights and benefits to same-sex couples.

CHOOSE ONE

Should same-sex marriage be legal?

YES ❑   NO ❑

Violence in Films, Television, and Video Games

Violence is common in films, television, and video games. Gratuitous violence is violence that is not necessary to the plot or that parents feel is inappropriate for their children.

FOR

Banning violence in films, television, and video games is censorship and a violation of First Amendment protections of free speech and expression. Parents who disapprove of violent entertainment should protect their children from it and let older youth and adults enjoy it if they wish.

AGAINST

Banning gratuitous violence in films, television, and video games is a safety issue. More and more children and young adults are committing copycat crimes inspired by the violence they have seen in films, television, and video games. Concerned parents believe such violence leaves an indelible impression on youth.

✔ CHOOSE ONE

Should gratuitous violence in films, television, and video games be allowed?

YES ❏   NO ❏

Entitlements
(Social Security and Welfare)

Social Security and welfare are considered entitlements, government programs that provide benefits to specific groups of people. Social Security pays retirement, disability, and survivors benefits to workers and their families. Welfare is financial assistance provided to people whose income falls below a certain level.

FOR

We are entitled to Social Security and welfare income because our taxes fund these programs. People count on Social Security to be there when they retire.

AGAINST

Entitlements breed laziness and complacency. Social Security is probably going to go bankrupt in another decade, and we could halve our tax burden by getting rid of public assistance altogether. Welfare subsidizes illegitimacy, encouraging young women to get pregnant in order to get welfare money.

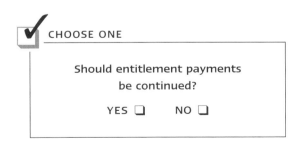

CHOOSE ONE

Should entitlement payments
be continued?

YES ☐   NO ☐

Flat Income Tax

Taxes are involuntary fees paid by individuals or businesses to a government. Income taxes are levied each year to pay for items such as military spending, national parks and highways, and welfare. Our current income tax system is progressive; that is, people pay different rates depending on their incomes and the deductions and credits for which they are eligible.

With a flat tax, everyone would pay the same percentage, as we do with other taxes such as the sales tax or gasoline tax. All deductions would be eliminated.

FOR

A straight flat tax with no deductions would mean no more arm-wrestling with tax forms, storing tax information for years, or hiring expensive accountants to interpret a complex tax code and to determine what is a legitimate deduction and what is not. As with the current income tax system, every American citizen and corporation in the United States or one of its territories would pay the tax.

AGAINST

With a flat tax, many would lose valuable deductions and business write-offs. A flat tax would also unfairly discriminate against the poor because they would pay the same percentage as the rich. In addition, the federal government uses the tax code to encourage behavior it wants more of, such as home buying or donating to charity. It would lose this power under a flat-tax system.

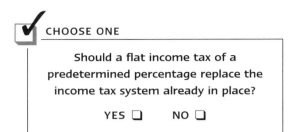

CHOOSE ONE

Should a flat income tax of a
predetermined percentage replace the
income tax system already in place?

YES ❏   NO ❏

National Debt

The national debt, which might better be termed the "federal debt," is the total amount of money the federal government has borrowed from institutions and individuals over the years and not yet repaid. The debt accumulates during years when the government spends more than it takes in. Like any borrower, the government has to pay interest on these loans.

FOR

Although it would be nice to reduce or eliminate the national debt, our government has nearly always carried some debt and our economy has always survived it. If the federal government requires additional capital in distressed periods, it should be allowed to borrow such funds.

AGAINST

The national debt should be eliminated. Just as we must be responsible for balancing our own checkbooks, so should the federal government be accountable to restrain its zealous overspending, balance its budget, and pay down the national debt.

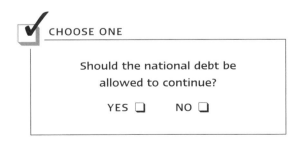

CHOOSE ONE

Should the national debt be allowed to continue?

YES ❑   NO ❑

National Lottery

A national lottery would be similar to a state lottery but operated by the federal government on a national level.

FOR

Instead of depending on the IRS, we could use a national lottery to raise hundreds of billions of dollars for vital government programs. Most states already have lotteries, and legalized gambling supports many institutions and communities all over the country, including Indian reservations and the state of Nevada.

AGAINST

The last thing we need in this country is more legalized gambling. Too many people already have problems controlling their gambling habits. We shouldn't count on a lottery to raise enough money to support our national security and other federal programs. A national lottery could be mismanaged.

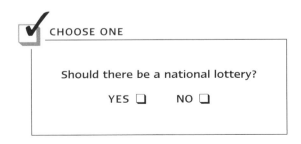

CHOOSE ONE

Should there be a national lottery?

YES ❑   NO ❑

National Sales Tax

A national sales tax (its percentage to be determined) is a consumption tax paid when someone buys something. It would replace income tax as a way to raise revenue for federal programs. We are used to paying state and local sales taxes for most purchases.

FOR

A national sales tax would eliminate the intrusive IRS and the complicated tax system we now have. Taxes would be paid at the cash register at the time of purchase, very similar to the VAT (value-added tax) in Great Britain. The states are already set up to collect sales taxes. They would collect an additional percentage for the national sales tax. A national sales tax would encourage people to save more of their income.

AGAINST

A national sales tax would hurt businesses and unfairly discriminate against the business community. Such a tax would devastate the economy. In addition, sales taxes discriminate against the poor, who spend a larger percentage of their income just to buy necessities.

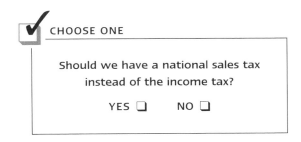

CHOOSE ONE

Should we have a national sales tax
instead of the income tax?

YES ❑   NO ❑

Foreign Aid

Foreign aid is the donation of money and supplies (medical, food, military) from our government to countries outside the United States.

FOR

It is paramount that we give vast quantities of funds, food, arms, and medicine to countries in need. Foreign aid not only helps the country in question, it also helps stabilize the rest of the world politically. Without foreign aid, many countries would dissolve into a welter of chaos and civil war that could have an impact outside their borders and destabilize entire regions. Israel is a good example. Without foreign aid, this vital Middle Eastern country would be in dire jeopardy.

AGAINST

Charity begins at home. Tens of thousands of people in this country are homeless and in want of food and shelter and basic provisions. Before the needs of others abroad are met, ours at home must first be taken care of. The billions of dollars that are sent overseas to assist people in other countries would be better spent on those who are in need in our own country.

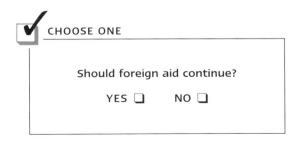

CHOOSE ONE

Should foreign aid continue?

YES ❑   NO ❑

Illegal Immigration

People who enter the United States without our government's knowledge or permission or stay beyond the termination date of their visas are engaging in illegal immigration. The most common form of illegal immigration is crossing over the U.S. border from either Canada or Mexico.

FOR

Workers come to this country illegally to work at jobs most American citizens do not want. However, these low-paying, labor-intensive jobs are crucial to our economy. Exceptions must be made to allow illegal immigrants to work in this country. Documents granting work rights and drivers' licenses should not be denied to immigrants just because of their illegal status.

AGAINST

Breaking any American law must not be tolerated. American citizens who unlawfully enter a foreign country are subject to deportation. Foreigners who enter the United States illegally should likewise be deported.

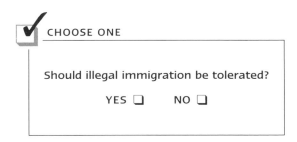

CHOOSE ONE

Should illegal immigration be tolerated?

YES ❑   NO ❑

The Wars in Iraq and Afghanistan

In an effort to combat terrorism, The United States is currently engaged in two wars abroad—one in Iraq, the other in Afghanistan.

FOR

Terrorism must be stamped out worldwide at all costs so that it never reaches U.S. borders. As a result of the efforts in Afghanistan and Iraq, we have not had a major terrorist attack in the United States since 9/11. In addition, the situation in the Middle East would quickly become much worse if we left now.

AGAINST

The two wars, now in their fourth year, have so far cost taxpayers over $400 billion.[11] This money would be better spent on security in the United States—for instance, strengthening our borders and enforcing immigration laws. In addition, over three thousand troops have died and more than twenty-five thousand have been injured so far.[12] Now that we are caught in a bloody civil war, more U.S. troops than ever before are perishing. Many high-ranking officials in the military are now conceding that this is going to be a long, drawn-out conflict, possibly taking years. We are only fanning the flames of this violence by our presence there.

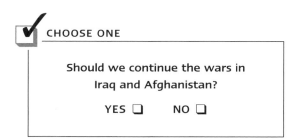

CHOOSE ONE

**Should we continue the wars in
Iraq and Afghanistan?**

YES ❑   NO ❑

Banning Guns

Banning guns is the most extreme form of gun control. While gun control restricts the purchase of certain types of firearms to certain individuals, banning prohibits the possession of all firearms except by military and law enforcement personnel.

FOR

We pay taxes for a police force for our protection. Law enforcement officials should be the ones who carry guns, not us. Many police and law enforcement officials believe that citizens who carry guns make their jobs dangerous.

The statistics speak for themselves: More than thirty thousand Americans were injured by firearms in 2002, according to the National Vital Statistics Report.[13] Guns are involved in thousands of senseless murders in this country every year. With easy access to firearms, students are killing students in schools throughout the nation. The shootings at Virginia Tech are just the latest example in a long series of tragedies. At home, children are accidentally killed by guns careless parents fail to lock up. According to the Centers for Disease Control and Prevention, firearms injuries remain a leading cause of death in the United States, particularly among youth.[14]

AGAINST

Banning guns won't help. Virginia Tech and Columbine High School were both "gun-free zones" when the shootings occurred.[15] The Second Amendment gives all American citizens the right to bear arms. Hunting and target shooting are popular pastimes. Guns are also indispensable for self-defense. States and communities that have adopted concealed weapons permits have seen a dramatic drop in their crime rates, particularly for violent crime.[16] Countless lives are saved each year by gun owners who use their weapons to protect themselves. In the time it can take woefully overburdened and understaffed local police forces to respond to a 911 emergency call, home invasion intruders, rapists, and murderers have already committed their crimes. The best defensive tool against these lethal threats is a gun.

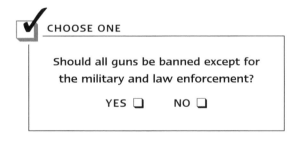

CHOOSE ONE

Should all guns be banned except for
the military and law enforcement?

YES ❏   NO ❏

Litigation Reform

When an individual or a corporation sues another party and loses the case, the party sued is responsible for paying all of its own legal fees and all of its out-of-pocket expenses. In a "loser pays" system, however, the loser of a lawsuit is required to pay all legal, court, and out-of-pocket costs for both parties.

FOR

"Loser pays" is the solution for our legal system because it would dramatically reduce the number of frivolous lawsuits.

AGAINST

"Loser pays" is unfair. People should be allowed to seek legal redress if they feel they have been wronged without having to worry about the financial consequences if they fail to get a judgment.

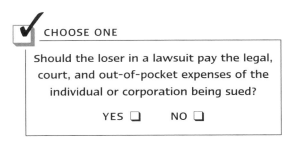

CHOOSE ONE

Should the loser in a lawsuit pay the legal, court, and out-of-pocket expenses of the individual or corporation being sued?

YES ☐   NO ☐

No-Knock Raids

On June 15, 2006, the Supreme Court ruled that police could forcibly enter homes without knocking or waiting.

FOR

Drug dealers and other lawbreakers should not be given any warning when police arrive because they will try to escape or destroy evidence. Police are required to get a special search warrant before they can enter a suspect's home unannounced.

AGAINST

Residents, fearing for their own lives and the safety of their family, could inadvertently shoot peace officers who fail to identify themselves. In November 2006, a ninety-two-year-old woman in Atlanta was shot by police in her home during a botched no-knock drug raid.[17] She later died.[18] Police have also burst into the wrong house by mistake.

✓ CHOOSE ONE

Should police be allowed to forcibly enter a home without identifying themselves?

YES ☐   NO ☐

Abortion

Abortion is the termination of a fetus. Abortions within the first trimester of pregnancy are called early abortions; abortions in the second or third trimester are called late-term abortions.

FOR

A woman has the right to choose abortion. As long as abortion is legal, as it now is, what she does with her body is completely up to her.

AGAINST

The willful termination of human life at any stage of pregnancy goes against God's will and constitutes murder.

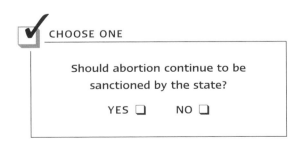

CHOOSE ONE

Should abortion continue to be
sanctioned by the state?

YES ❏   NO ❏

Capital Punishment

When a person commits a heinous crime such as first-degree murder or treason, the offense might warrant "special circumstances," which means that the state can take the life of that individual by execution.

FOR

Capital punishment deters potential murderers. It protects innocent people by eliminating the most violent criminals, and it helps victims' families by providing retribution. Capital punishment shows criminals that one pays a price for serious wrongdoing.

AGAINST

Taking a person's life in retribution for a crime is just as barbaric and inhumane as the original crime and is itself murder. On its Web page entitled "Facts about Deterrence and the Death Penalty," the Death Penalty Information Center, a nonprofit organization that studies issues pertaining to capital punishment, cites myriad studies that attest to the fact that capital punishment does not deter crime.[19] Life is sacred; mistakes are made and innocent people are executed. Life imprisonment without the possibility of parole is a much more appropriate sentence than the death penalty even for the crime of murder.

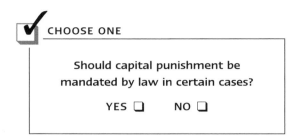

CHOOSE ONE

Should capital punishment be
mandated by law in certain cases?

YES ☐   NO ☐

Universal Healthcare

A universal healthcare system ensures that all citizens receive complete healthcare and all necessary medications without any direct costs to them. Such a system would be government run and funded by taxes, similar to Medicare.

FOR

Universal healthcare is a system that is long overdue in our country to ease the financial strain of medical expenses shouldered by millions of Americans. In a 2003 ABCNews/ *Washington Post* poll, Americans preferred a universal health insurance program over the current employer-based system by a 2–1 margin. While it is true that taxes would have to be raised, the money that would fund the program could come from a variety of sources, not just personal income taxes. The British National Health Service, for instance, is funded jointly by a health insurance tax and by the national treasury.[20] In our country, 50 percent of all consumer bankruptcies are triggered by health-related issues.[21] This is just one way that, as a society, we pay a high cost for not providing healthcare for all citizens.

AGAINST

Our current system isn't perfect, but a universal healthcare plan would burden our economy. Taxes would soar in order to fund this plan. It is possible that without the economic incentive that now motivates many drug makers, medical research and innovation would dry up altogether.[22] In addition, universal healthcare would probably mean that people would have a limited choice of doctors and longer waits for care. The 2003 ABCNews/*Washington Post* survey found that fewer than four out of ten Americans support universal healthcare if it means waiting lists for nonemergency treatment or a limited choice of doctors.[23]

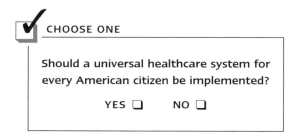

CHOOSE ONE

Should a universal healthcare system for every American citizen be implemented?

YES ☐   NO ☐

Voluntary Euthanasia

Voluntary euthanasia, also called assisted dying, means that a competent adult suffering unbearably from an incurable illness, whose quality of life has become severely compromised, may request and receive medical help to die. Oregon passed a "physician-assisted suicide" law in 1997. It was upheld by the U.S. Supreme Court in 2006.[24] However, voluntary euthanasia is not legal in the rest of the United States.

FOR

Issues of mortality are entirely up to each person to determine. If someone's quality of life is diminished by terminal illness, the decision to die belongs to the individual, not the government.

AGAINST

Legalizing voluntary euthanasia will encourage unscrupulous doctors who can abuse their power by "euthanizing" people inappropriately. Family members might also be tempted to take advantage of an elderly relative. From a legal perspective, voluntary euthanasia is the willful taking of a human life no matter what the patient's condition. It is tantamount to murder. From a religious perspective, when life should end is not up to the individual but to God.

Should voluntary euthanasia be legal?

YES ❑   NO ❑

Take Action!

Congratulations. You have just reviewed and voted on the most important issues facing our country. Tear out the perforated ballot at the end of the book or photocopy the following voter ballot. Mark your choices in ink and send it to

**The President of the United States of America
The White House
1600 Pennsylvania Avenue NW
Washington, DC 20500**

You can also vote online at

http://www.howwouldyouvote.us

Remember, these are your wishes. We need to remind the president that he (or she) must listen to the people of this country.

SELECT YES OR NO FOR EACH ISSUE BY FILLING IN THE APPROPRIATE CIRCLE. WRITE YOUR
NAME AND ADDRESS ON THE OTHER SIDE AND MAIL TO THE PRESIDENT.

DEMOCRACY & GOVERNMENT

CONSTITUTIONAL AMENDMENTS Should changes
or further amendments to the Constitution of the
United States of America be allowed by law?
YES ○ NO ○

DEMOCRACY Should America become a democracy?
YES ○ NO ○

THE ELECTORAL COLLEGE Should the United
States continue to use the Electoral College system
to choose its president? YES ○ NO ○

**PENSIONS FOR POLITICIANS AND FEDERAL
EMPLOYEES** Should federal workers and politicians
have lifetime pensions? YES ○ NO ○

CITIZENS' RIGHTS & RESPONSIBILITIES

AFFIRMATIVE ACTION Should affirmative action
policies, which give preferential treatment based on
minority status, be protected? YES ○ NO ○

EMINENT DOMAIN Should private property be
forcibly taken and sold for the use of private
urban development? YES ○ NO ○

FREE SPEECH Should freedom of speech always be
protected? YES ○ NO ○

MANDATORY NATIONAL SERVICE Should
national service be mandatory? YES ○ NO ○

NATIONAL IDENTITY CARD Should every
American citizen be required to have a national
identity card? YES ○ NO ○

NATIONAL LANGUAGE Should a single national
language, English, be instituted for the country's
official communications? YES ○ NO ○

PERSONAL LIBERTY

ALCOHOL AND TOBACCO PROHIBITION Should
alcohol and tobacco be prohibited? YES ○ NO ○

NARCOTICS DECRIMINALIZATION Should narcotics be decriminalized? YES ○ NO ○

PORNOGRAPHY Should pornography be legal?
YES ○ NO ○

PROSTITUTION Should prostitution be legal?
YES ○ NO ○

SAME-SEX MARRIAGE Should same-sex marriage
be legal? YES ○ NO ○

**VIOLENCE IN FILMS, TELEVISION, AND VIDEO
GAMES** Should gratuitous violence in films, television, and video games be allowed? YES ○ NO ○

TAXES & SPENDING

**ENTITLEMENTS (SOCIAL SECURITY AND
WELFARE)** Should entitlement payments be
continued? YES ○ NO ○

FLAT INCOME TAX Should a flat income tax of a
predetermined percentage replace the income tax
system already in place? YES ○ NO ○

NATIONAL DEBT Should the national debt be
allowed to continue? YES ○ NO ○

NATIONAL LOTTERY Should there be a national
lottery? YES ○ NO ○

NATIONAL SALES TAX Should we have a national
sales tax instead of the income tax?
YES ○ NO ○

INTERNATIONAL ISSUES

FOREIGN AID Should foreign aid continue?
YES ○ NO ○

ILLEGAL IMMIGRATION Should illegal immigration be tolerated? YES ○ NO ○

THE WARS IN IRAQ AND AFGHANISTAN
Should we continue the wars in Iraq and
Afghanistan? YES ○ NO ○

LAW & ORDER

BANNING GUNS Should all guns be banned
except for the military and law enforcement?
YES ○ NO ○

LITIGATION REFORM Should the loser in a
lawsuit pay the legal, court, and out-of-pocket
expenses of the individual or corporation being
sued? YES ○ NO ○

NO-KNOCK RAIDS Should police be allowed to
forcibly enter a home without identifying themselves? YES ○ NO ○

LIFE & DEATH ISSUES

ABORTION Should abortion continue to be
sanctioned by the state? YES ○ NO ○

CAPITAL PUNISHMENT Should capital
punishment be mandated by law in certain cases?
YES ○ NO ○

UNIVERSAL HEALTHCARE Should a universal
healthcare system for every American citizen be
implemented? YES ○ NO ○

VOLUNTARY EUTHANASIA Should voluntary
euthanasia be legal? YES ○ NO ○

The President of the United States

The White House

1600 Pennsylvania Avenue NW

Washington, DC 20500

Name: _____

Address: _____

_____

Dear Mr./Mdm. President,

Please review my ballot and then deliver it to the Government Accountability Office to be tabulated with the others like it. Whatever the outcome of the vote, we demand that our wishes be enacted into law.

EPILOGUE

A Final Word

Stop for a moment and think. What would it be like to live in a country where every vote mattered? What would it be like if our government was not just for the people but truly by the people? What would it be like to live in a democracy?

With national voting we will vote on measures directly, instead of counting on a representative to do it for us and hoping he or she does what we want. National voting is a democracy that we can all participate in. It will make people think and make them act.

National voting levels the playing field because everyone's vote is equal. It cuts out special interests. It protects our vote by ensuring that it will become law for ten years. It resolves all the issues once and for all and thereby creates tremendous peace of mind.

Now we are faced with making the most important decision of our lives. Ahead of us lies self-determination. For the first time in our history we have to decide whether it is better to make decisions for ourselves or whether others should make decisions for us. We must now decide whether to adopt democracy or continue living in a republic.

All of the great movements in our country began with a simple idea. But the one simple idea that we have overlooked is by far the most important: democracy.

A journey of a thousand miles begins with a single step. And that first step is our vote. Each and every one of us must vote because this is the journey of democracy. We must make this journey alone, without the help of politicians and courts. Only we can decide the issues for ourselves. Only we can vote on the issues because they are far too important to be left to the politicians or the courts.

When we place our hands on our hearts and recite the phrase "and to the Republic for which it stands," we must remind ourselves that it represents a world that no longer works, one that we must now say good-bye to. When we embrace national voting, that phrase will be permanently changed to "and to the Democracy for which it stands."

Remember that this country does not belong to the politicians, the lobbyists, or the special interest groups. It does not belong to the Supreme Court, or any court, for that matter. It belongs to you.

APPENDICES

In this section you'll find a list of Internet resources to help you find out what our government is really up to. Once we get national voting, information like this will be crucial when we make our decisions.

You'll also find out how to contact your congressional representative and tell him or her what your decision is about the issues that matter.

APPENDIX A
RESOURCES

Until we the people take back our power with national voting, we need to learn as much as we can about our current political system and keep a close eye on our elected officials. Technology is making it much easier to find out what's really going on in Washington. For the first time we the people are getting a peek at what goes on behind the closed doors of power.

As you know, the Internet has an overwhelming number of Web sites with information about our political system. If you are interested enough to be reading this book, you probably already have some favorites. The sites listed here all provide lots of valuable insight into our government and the politicians who claim to represent us. Some are sponsored by the federal government (those with .gov in their domain names); some, by citizens groups. Many were referred to in the writing of this book.

Center for Media and Democracy
http://www.prwatch.org/cmd/index.html
This nonpartisan public interest organization reports on behind-the-scenes public relations campaigns by corporations, industries, governments, and other powerful institutions. From here

you can explore SourceWatch, a directory of people, organizations, and issues shaping the public agenda; Congresspedia, the "citizen's encyclopedia on Congress"; and other related sites.

Center for Public Integrity

http://www.publicintegrity.org/lobby/

Use this searchable database to learn more about who's lobbying and why. Search by industry, issue, state, country, or agency. Find the top companies and organizations and the top lobbying firms plus an easy-to-understand explanation about the rules for lobbying.

Federal Judiciary

http://www.uscourts.gov/

Find information about the judicial branch of the U.S. government: the Supreme Court, the U.S. Courts of Appeals, the District Courts, and the Bankruptcy Courts.

GovTrack

http://www.govtrack.us/

This independent site, run by a graduate student, brings together lots of information about the United States Congress and tracks the status of federal legislation and the activities of your senators and representatives. Research legislation, find out what legislation is being blogged about, or sign up for e-mail updates and RSS feeds.

Historical Documents

http://www.house.gov/house/Educate.shtml
http://memory.loc.gov/ammem/help/constRedir.html

You'll find important historical documents here, including early congressional documents, the Federalist Papers, and primary documents from every period of our history.

The Library of Unified Information Sources
http://www.louisdb.org/about/
This new project of the Sunlight Foundation is working to create a comprehensive, completely indexed, and cross-referenced depository of federal documents from the executive and legislative branches of government. For example, in the Presidential Documents section, you'll find information about presidential appointments, executive orders, and speeches.

Lobby Filing Disclosure Program
http://sopr.senate.gov/
This site from the U.S. Senate and the Office of Public Records allows the public to view filings about lobbyists and their clients.

MAPLight
http://www.MAPLight.org
This public database highlights the connection between money and politics. It combines data about campaign contributions and how legislators vote. Originally covering California legislators only, the site recently expanded to cover the U.S. Congress as well.

The National Archives
http://www.archives.gov/national-archives-experience /charters/charters.html
Here you'll find copies of our country's most important documents—the Declaration of Independence and the Constitution,

with all its amendments. If you haven't read these documents in a while, take a look at them. You'll probably find at least a few passages that will astound you.

Office of the Clerk of the U.S. House of Representatives
http://clerk.house.gov/
If you want to learn more about the U.S. House of Representatives, start here.

OMB Watch
http://www.ombwatch.org/
This Washington, DC–based organization works to increase transparency and accountability in the federal government. You can begin here to explore several related sites sponsored by this group.

Open Congress
http://www.opencongress.org/
Find out what your senators and congressional representatives are really up to. This site combines official government data with news and blog coverage to give you the real story behind each bill.

Open Secrets
http://www.opensecrets.org/
The lobbying database on this site lets you find the top spenders by industry or issue as well as the top donors to political campaigns. You'll also find databases that show who the richest members of Congress are, who takes the most sponsored trips, and who's moving back and forth from the public to the private sector.

OpenTheGovernment.org

http://www.openthegovernment.org/

This coalition of consumer and good-government groups, environmentalists, journalists, library groups, labor, and others is working to make the federal government more open in order to make us safer, strengthen public trust in government, and support our democratic principles.

The Project on Government Oversight

http://pogo.org

POGO (formerly known as Project on Military Procurement) originally worked to expose outrageous military spending such as the $7,600 coffee maker and the $436 hammer. After many successes reforming the military, POGO now investigates waste, fraud, and abuse in all federal agencies.

Sunlight Foundation

http://www.sunlightfoundation.com

The Sunlight Foundation uses information technology to help citizens to learn more about what their elected representatives are doing. If you're really passionate about a particular issue in Congress, you can even sign up for a Twitter feed about it.

Thomas

http://thomas.loc.gov/

In the spirit of Thomas Jefferson, the Library of Congress provides legislative information about both the Senate and the House of Representatives, including bills, resolutions, treaties, committee reports, the Congressional Record, and roll call votes.

U.S. National Debt Clock

http://www.brillig.com/debt_clock/

This site features an up-to-date total of the national debt and shows how much each person's share amounts to.

U.S. Senate

http://senate.gov/

Find out who your senators are, what committees they sit on, and what legislation is working its way through the senate.

U.S. Supreme Court

http://www.supremecourtus.gov/

Find recent decisions, the Court calendar, information about Court procedures, and a database of Supreme Court decisions since 1893.

U.S. Treasury and the National Debt

http://www.treasurydirect.gov/govt/resources/faq
/faq_publicdebt.htm

This U.S. Treasury site answers FAQs about the national debt.

APPENDIX B
HOW TO CONTACT YOUR ELECTED OFFICIALS

For now we live in a republic, not a democracy. Our representatives get to make the decisions for us. Until we can make the decisions for ourselves, we need to let them know what we think.

The first step is to find out who your senators and representatives are. Your local newspaper probably has this information, perhaps in the editorial pages. The white pages of your phone book probably have a government section that lists senators and representatives for your area. If you live in a metropolitan area with several representatives, however, the phone book may not tell you which one represents your district. The easiest way to find out who represents you is to go to one of the following Web sites.

SENATORS

Start at http://senate.gov/. Choose your state from the pull-down menu, and you'll find a Web form to use to send an e-mail to either of your state's two senators plus links to their Web sites. Their Web sites will give you mailing addresses, phone numbers, and fax numbers for both their Washington and local offices.

Keep in mind that new security procedures for mail handling in government office buildings can delay mail for weeks or even months. Faxes, phone calls, or e-mail messages are probably better choices. The address on a letter to a senator begins like this: "The Honorable John Doe." You can begin your message with "Dear Senator Doe."

CONGRESSIONAL REPRESENTATIVES

Here are two Web sites you can use to find out who represents your district and how to contact him or her:

- GovTrack (http://www.govtrack.us) lets you find out what congressional district you're in by zooming in on a Google map. You'll find a link to the representative's Web site, which will give you ways to contact him or her by phone, fax, mail, or e-mail.
- Write Your Representative (http://www.house.gov/writerep) lets you find your representative by zip code. You'll need to enter the four-digit extension too, but the site tells you how to look it up if you don't know it. Once you know who your representative is, you'll find a form that makes it easy to send him or her an e-mail.

Note that some representatives require you to be a resident of their district to write to them, and most request that you include your mailing address and your e-mail address in your message, at least if you want a reply.

Keep in mind that new security procedures for mail handling in government office buildings can delay mail for weeks or even months. Faxes, phone calls, or e-mail messages are probably better choices.

The address on a letter to a representative begins like this: "The Honorable Jane Doe." Your message should start with "Dear Representative Doe" or "Dear Ms. Doe."

SUPREME COURT

In addition to your senators and representative, you can contact a Supreme Court justice using this address: Public Information Officer, Supreme Court of the United States, Washington, DC 20543. You can phone the Supreme Court's Public Information Office at (202) 479-3211.

NOTES

Preface

1. C-SPAN, "Election of 2000: The Civics Lesson of the New Century," http://www.c-span.org/classroom/govt/2000.asp.

Part 1 National Voting: Power to the People
Chapter 1: It's Time for a Second American Revolution

1. U.S. Census Bureau, "Voting and Registration in the Election of November 2004: Population Characteristics," March 2006, 14, http://www.census.gov/prod/2006pubs /p20-556.pdf.
2. Ibid., 11.
3. "Judge Voids Calif. Proposition on Immigrants," *Washington Post*, March 19, 1998.
4. Wendy Koch, "'Go-getter,' 18, Ousts Mayor in Michigan," *USA Today*, November 9, 2005.
5. C-SPAN, "Election of 2000: The Civics Lesson of the New Century," http://www.c-span.org/classroom/govt /2000.asp.
6. *Merriam-Webster's Collegiate Dictionary*, 11th ed., s.v. "republic."
7. CNN.com, "How We Got Here: A Timeline of the Florida Recount," December 13, 2000, http://archives.cnn.com /2000/ALLPOLITICS/stories/12/13/got.here/index.html.

Chapter 2: Americans and Voting: A Love Story

1. Nichola Groom, "Jordin Sparks Becomes Youngest 'Idol' Winner," Reuters, May 24, 2007. http://www.reuters.com /article/newsOne/idUSN2325859920070524.

2. Mark Sweney, "American Idol Outvotes the President," *Guardian*, May 26, 2006, http://www.guardian.co.uk /international/story/0,,1783339,00.html.

3. Bret Hovell, "'Idol' Voters Have Faith in Their Vote," ABC News, May 4, 2006, http://abcnews.go.com/Entertainment /story?id=1923394.

4. Ethan J. Leib, "Why Not Dial-In Democracy, Too?" *Washington Post*, May 28, 2006, http://www.washington post.com/wpdyn/content/article/2006/05/26/AR2006052601 711_pf.html.

5. Calvin R. Trice, "Here's Proof Each Vote Counts," *Richmond (VA) Times-Dispatch*, November 10, 2005.

6. Central Intelligence Agency, "The World Factbook," https://www.cia.gov/library/publications/the-world-factbook/geos/us.html#People, accessed August 1, 2007.

7. Elizabeth Brown, "Lobbying FAQ: What Is Permissible? Out of Bounds? Punishable?" LobbyWatch, The Center for Public Integrity, http://www.publicintegrity.org /lobby /report.aspx?aid=775.

8. "Committee Reports: 110th Congress," Library of Congress, Thomas, http://thomas.loc.gov/cp110/cp110 query.html.

9. Will Bunch, "Why the Levee Broke," Alternet, September 1, 2005, http://www.alternet.org.

10. Andrew Martin and Andrew Zajac, "Flood-Control Funds Short of Requests," *Chicago Tribune*, September 1, 2005.

11. Phil Keisling, "Election Fraud, American Style," *Washington Monthly*, December 2006.

12. Barbara Mikkelson, "'One Vote' Fallacies," Snopes.com, http://www.snopes.com/history/govern/onevote.htm.

13. Andy Rooney, "Let's Vote . . . On Everything!" *60 Minutes*, February 18, 2007.

Chapter 3: Thinking Outside the Ballot Box

1. Ace Project, "Swiss Direct Democracy," Ace Focus on Direct Democracy, http://www.focus.aceproject.org/direct-democracy/cs-swiss.

2. League of Women Voters of Massachusetts, "Your Vote Makes a Difference," http://www.ma.lwv.org/Election Pubs/your_vote.htm.

3. *Brainy Encyclopedia*, s.v. "direct democracy," http://www .brainyencyclopedia.com/encyclopedia/d/di/direct%5f democracy.html.

4. Medical Board of California, "Medical Marijuana," May 7, 2004, http://www.medbd.ca.gov/Medical_Marijuana.htm.

5. Peggy Lowe, "Janet Nguyen Named Supervisor," *Orange County (CA) Register*, March 26, 2007. http://www.oc register.com/ocregister/homepage/abox/article_1631823 .php.

6. Rhonda Grussendorf, interview with the author, *Help Me Rhonda Show*, KDAL-AM (Duluth, MN), September 12, 2006.

Chapter 4: We've Got the Smarts to Do It Ourselves

1. Seth Mandel, "Farkas Wins Council Seat—By One Vote," *East Brunswick (NJ) Sentinel*, November 23, 2005.

2. Seth Mandel, "Election Tally Reverses; Cruz Wins by One Vote," *East Brunswick (NJ) Sentinel*, December 1, 2005.

3. National Court Reporters Association, "Grass Roots Lobbying," http://www.ncraonline.org/ppa/grassroots /vote .shtml.

Chapter 5: What Would Change—and What Wouldn't

1. Warren Richey, "Court Sides with Police in Restraining Order Case," *Christian Science Monitor*, June 28, 2005. http://www.csmonitor.com/2005/0628/p25s01-usju.html.

2. Andrew Ferguson, "Convenience Voting: The End of Election Day," *Weekly Standard*, November 20, 2006.

3. National Court Reporters Association, "Grass Roots Lobbying," http://www.ncraonline.org/ppa/grassroots /vote.shtml.

4. Ariel J. Feldman, J. Alex Halderman, and Edward W. Felten, "Security Analysis of the Diebold AccuVote-TS Voting Machine," Center for Information Technology Policy, September 13, 2006, http://itpolicy.princeton.edu /voting/summary.html.

5. National Court Reporters Association, "Grass Roots Lobbying," http://www.ncraonline.org/ppa/grassroots/vote .shtml.

6. Thomas Jefferson, "On the Need for a Little Rebellion Now and Then," *Britannica*, http://www.britannica.com /presidents/article-9116911.

Part 2 The Issues: Make Your Voice Heard

1. *Encyclopedia Americana*, s.v. "Electoral College," http:// ap.grolier.com/article?assetid=0140130-00&template name=/article/article.html.

2. Patrick J. Purcell, "Retirement Benefits for Members of Congress," Congressional Research Service, February 9, 2007, http://www.senate.gov/reference/resources/pdf /RL30631.pdf.

3. Charles Lane, "Justices Affirm Property Seizures," *Washington Post*, June 24, 2005, http://www.washingtonpost.com /wpdyn/content/article/2005/06/23/AR2005062300783.html.

4. Mothers Against Drunk Driving, "Statistics," http://www .madd.org/stats/1112, accessed August 2, 2007.

5. Mothers Against Drunk Driving, "Statistics," http://www .madd.org/stats/9659, accessed August 2, 2007.

6. Centers for Disease Control and Prevention, "Cigarette Smoking-Attributable Morbidity—United States 2000," *Morbidity and Mortality Weekly Report* 52, no. 35

(September 5, 2003), http://www.cdc.gov/tobacco/data_statistics/MMWR/20.

7. DrugSense, "Drug War Clock," drugsense.org, http://www.drugsense.org/wodclock.htm, accessed August 2, 2007.

8. Marianne Szegedy-Maszak, "Ensnared," *Los Angeles Times*, December 26, 2005.

9. Bureau of Democracy, Human Rights, and Labor, "Country Reports on Human Rights Practices: The Netherlands," February 25, 2004, U.S. Department of State, http://www.state.gov/g/drl/rls/hrrpt/2003 /27856.htm.

10. Gary Langer, with Cheryl Arnedt and Dalia Sussman, "Primetime Live Poll: American Sex Survey," October 21, 2004, http://abcnews.go.com/Primetime/News/Story?id=156921&page=1.

11. National Priorities Project, "The War in Iraq Costs," http://costofwar.com/, accessed August 2, 2007.

12. Iraq Coalition Casualty Count, http://icasualties.org/oif/, accessed August 2, 2007.

13. Centers for Disease Control and Prevention, *National Vital Statistics Report* 53, no. 5 (October 12, 2004)

14. Ibid.

15. John R. Lott Jr., "Bans Don't Deter Killers," *USA Today*, April 23, 2007, http://johnrlott.tripod.com/op-eds/USA TodayGunFreeZones042307.html.

16. John R. Lott Jr., *Straight Shooting: Firearms, Economics, and Public Policy* (Bellevue, WA: Merril Press, 2006), 72.

17. Ronda Cook, "Atlanta Police Indicted in Fatal Drug Raid," *Atlanta Journal-Constitution*, April 26, 2007.

18. "Police: Shooting of Elderly Woman 'Tragic, Unfortunate'" WSB-TV, November 21, 2006, http://www.wsbtv.com/news /10374909/detail.html.

19. Death Penalty Information Center, "Facts about Deterrence and the Death Penalty," http://www.deathpenaltyinfo.org /article.php?scid=12&did=167#STUDIES.

20. *Columbia Encyclopedia*, s.v. "socialized medicine," http://www.answers.com/topic/publicly-funded-medicine.

21. Liz Pulliam Weston, "Big Medical Bills Sometimes Make Bankruptcy Necessary," *Los Angeles Times*, July 28, 2005.

22. Alicia Chang, "Drug Companies Influence Research," *Madison (WI) Capital Times*, May 26, 2005. Chang notes that private industry funds more than two-thirds of the medical research done at U.S. universities.

23. Gary Langer, "Health Care Pains: Growing Health Care Concerns Fuel Cautious Support for Change," ABC News, October 20, 2003, http://abcnews.go.com/sections/living/US/healthcare031020_poll.html.

24. Death with Dignity National Center, "Chronology of Assisted Dying," http://www.deathwithdignity.org/history facts/chronology.asp.

INDEX

U.S. Supreme Court
    ability to overrule electoral
        votes, 6
    eminent domain ruling, 51
    justices of, 12, 35, 119
    no-knock raids ruling, 93
    physician-assisted suicide
        ruling, 101
USA Today, 9

V

violence in films/games/television,
    71
Virginia Tech, 89
voluntary euthanasia, 101–102
voter identification numbers,
    27
voting. *See also* national voting
    absentee, 35
    in democracies, 6
    online, 30
    phone, 30
    protection of, 37–38
    reasons for not, 4–5
    technology, 10, 35–37

voting machines
    accuracy of, 4
    Diebold AccuVote-TS paperless,
        36
    sabotage of, 36
voting systems
    fairness of, 5
    problems of U.S., 4–5
    winner-take-all, 3

W

Wall Street Journal, 9
warrantless searches, 93
wars, Iraq/Afghanistan, 87–88
Washington Post, 10, 99, 100
Web sites
    agencies/resources, 111–116
    government officials', 117–119
    voting online, 103
welfare, 73
Wick, Hal, 37
Williams, Robin, 36
winner-take-all voting systems, 3
Wyman, Louis, 18

ABOUT THE AUTHOR

W. R. WILKERSON III is a songwriter and the author of *How Would You Vote If You Were Allowed To?* (Ciro's Books, 2006); *The Man Who Invented Las Vegas* (Ciro's Books, 2000); *All-American Ads of the 40s*, edited by Jim Heimann (Taschen, 2002); *Las Vegas: Vintage Graphics from Sin City* (Taschen, 2003); and *The Monk's Son* (Ciro's Books, 2007). His Web site is www.howwouldyouvote.us.

SELECT YES OR NO FOR EACH ISSUE BY FILLING IN THE APPROPRIATE CIRCLE. WRITE YOUR
NAME AND ADDRESS ON THE OTHER SIDE AND MAIL TO THE PRESIDENT.

DEMOCRACY & GOVERNMENT

CONSTITUTIONAL AMENDMENTS Should changes or further amendments to the Constitution of the United States of America be allowed by law? YES ◯ NO ◯

DEMOCRACY Should America become a democracy? YES ◯ NO ◯

THE ELECTORAL COLLEGE Should the United States continue to use the Electoral College system to choose its president? YES ◯ NO ◯

PENSIONS FOR POLITICIANS AND FEDERAL EMPLOYEES Should federal workers and politicians have lifetime pensions? YES ◯ NO ◯

CITIZENS' RIGHTS & RESPONSIBILITIES

AFFIRMATIVE ACTION Should affirmative action policies, which give preferential treatment based on minority status, be protected? YES ◯ NO ◯

EMINENT DOMAIN Should private property be forcibly taken and sold for the use of private urban development? YES ◯ NO ◯

FREE SPEECH Should freedom of speech always be protected? YES ◯ NO ◯

MANDATORY NATIONAL SERVICE Should national service be mandatory? YES ◯ NO ◯

NATIONAL IDENTITY CARD Should every American citizen be required to have a national identity card? YES ◯ NO ◯

NATIONAL LANGUAGE Should a single national language, English, be instituted for the country's official communications? YES ◯ NO ◯

PERSONAL LIBERTY

ALCOHOL AND TOBACCO PROHIBITION Should alcohol and tobacco be prohibited? YES ◯ NO ◯

NARCOTICS DECRIMINALIZATION Should narcotics be decriminalized? YES ◯ NO ◯

PORNOGRAPHY Should pornography be legal? YES ◯ NO ◯

PROSTITUTION Should prostitution be legal? YES ◯ NO ◯

SAME-SEX MARRIAGE Should same-sex marriage be legal? YES ◯ NO ◯

VIOLENCE IN FILMS, TELEVISION, AND VIDEO GAMES Should gratuitous violence in films, television, and video games be allowed? YES ◯ NO ◯

TAXES & SPENDING

ENTITLEMENTS (SOCIAL SECURITY AND WELFARE) Should entitlement payments be continued? YES ◯ NO ◯

FLAT INCOME TAX Should a flat income tax of a predetermined percentage replace the income tax system already in place? YES ◯ NO ◯

NATIONAL DEBT Should the national debt be allowed to continue? YES ◯ NO ◯

NATIONAL LOTTERY Should there be a national lottery? YES ◯ NO ◯

NATIONAL SALES TAX Should we have a national sales tax instead of the income tax? YES ◯ NO ◯

INTERNATIONAL ISSUES

FOREIGN AID Should foreign aid continue? YES ◯ NO ◯

ILLEGAL IMMIGRATION Should illegal immigration be tolerated? YES ◯ NO ◯

THE WARS IN IRAQ AND AFGHANISTAN Should we continue the wars in Iraq and Afghanistan? YES ◯ NO ◯

LAW & ORDER

BANNING GUNS Should all guns be banned except for the military and law enforcement? YES ◯ NO ◯

LITIGATION REFORM Should the loser in a lawsuit pay the legal, court, and out-of-pocket expenses of the individual or corporation being sued? YES ◯ NO ◯

NO-KNOCK RAIDS Should police be allowed to forcibly enter a home without identifying themselves? YES ◯ NO ◯

LIFE & DEATH ISSUES

ABORTION Should abortion continue to be sanctioned by the state? YES ◯ NO ◯

CAPITAL PUNISHMENT Should capital punishment be mandated by law in certain cases? YES ◯ NO ◯

UNIVERSAL HEALTHCARE Should a universal healthcare system for every American citizen be implemented? YES ◯ NO ◯

VOLUNTARY EUTHANASIA Should voluntary euthanasia be legal? YES ◯ NO ◯

One Person, One Vote by W. R. Wilkerson III © 2008

The President of the United States

The White House

1600 Pennsylvania Avenue NW

Washington, DC 20500

Name: _____

Address: _____

Dear Mr./Mdm. President,

Please review my ballot and then deliver it to the Government Accountability Office to be tabulated with the others like it. Whatever the outcome of the vote, we demand that our wishes be enacted into law.